# A CHILD'S BOOK OF

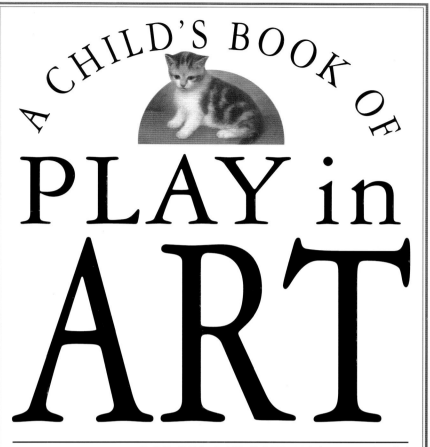

# PLAY in ART

SELECTED BY LUCY MICKLETHWAIT

## GREAT PICTURES
## GREAT FUN

## DORLING KINDERSLEY

LONDON • NEW YORK • STUTTGART • MOSCOW

A DORLING KINDERSLEY BOOK

*For my mother*
*and father*

**Editor** Rachel Harrison
**Designer** Sarah Thornton
**Managing Editor** Sheila Hanly
**DTP Designer** Nicola Studdart
**Picture Researcher** Jo Carlill
**Production** Louise Barratt

First published in Great Britain in 1996
by Dorling Kindersley Limited,
9 Henrietta Street, London WC2E 8PS

Reproduced in Italy by G.R.B. Graphica, Verona
Printed and bound in Italy by Mondadori

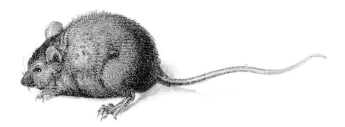

# Contents

Note to Parents
and Teachers 8

Let's Play 10
All Dressed Up 12

Where Shall We Live? 14
Let's Pretend 16

Make the Faces 18
Animal Noises 20

Crazy Creatures 32
Crazy Colours 34

How Do They Smell? 22
How Do They Taste? 24

Make up a Story 36
Spot the Difference 38

Copy the Patterns 26
Touch and Feel 28
Match the Animals 30

What Shall
We Do Next? 40
Picture List 42

# Note to Parents and Teachers

**I**ntroducing children to art is as easy as opening a book, and the rewards are enormous. For thousands of years people have expressed themselves through art, so there is much to see and a great deal to learn. By giving children just a few pictures, you can open up this world of infinite richness and diversity for them to explore.

**A**s you look at these pictures with a child, talk about anything that springs to mind – the expression on a face, the pattern on a dress, or even the colour of the sky. Talk about how a picture makes you both feel. Is it a happy picture or a sad one? Is it noisy or quiet? Imagine that you can climb right into the pictures together – rolling hoops in a playground scene or defending a castle under siege.

**I** have chosen pictures that will, I hope, inspire a wide range of activities. Children can pretend to be angry like the Japanese actor, or fast asleep like the princess. They can have fun dressing up as knights in armour, they can make animal noises, or copy the different faces.

**Q**uieter activities include matching games, which are fun and encourage close observation. Children can match cut-out details to the pictures – a peacock from an animal painting, or a child skipping from a Japanese print. Another game, "Spot the Difference", where children can compare old and new versions of the same scene, requires even closer scrutiny.

The paintings in this book offer endless opportunities for broadening a child's general knowledge. Point out different styles of architecture and costume, talk about the Aztecs and the Greeks, or compare the Iowa chief with the young Queen Elizabeth. Some paintings, such as those illustrating the five senses, can be used specifically to develop a child's vocabulary. Others can be used to develop the imagination; ask the child to imagine what people are thinking, or to make up a story about a favourite picture.

All artists are influenced and inspired by one another. Some children may like to copy a painting, or trace it and colour it in. Others may like to paint their own funny-coloured animals or invent some crazy ones of their own. Experimenting with patterns and designs is always fun; the Aboriginal diamond design would work well with wax crayons and watercolour, and Klimt's patchwork cloak could inspire a lovely collage of coloured paper and sweet wrappers. All such activities are not only entertaining, but also help to increase a child's understanding of art.

You do not need to be a teacher or an art historian to share a painting with a child. Children love exploring pictures and finding in them familiar and unfamiliar things. Let them guide you through this book and share with them the delight of discovering something new on every page.

Lucy Micklethwait

# Let's Play

*Children's Games*, 1560, Pieter Bruegel the Elder

tug-of-war

leap-frog

headstand

rolling hoops

riding a
hobby-horse

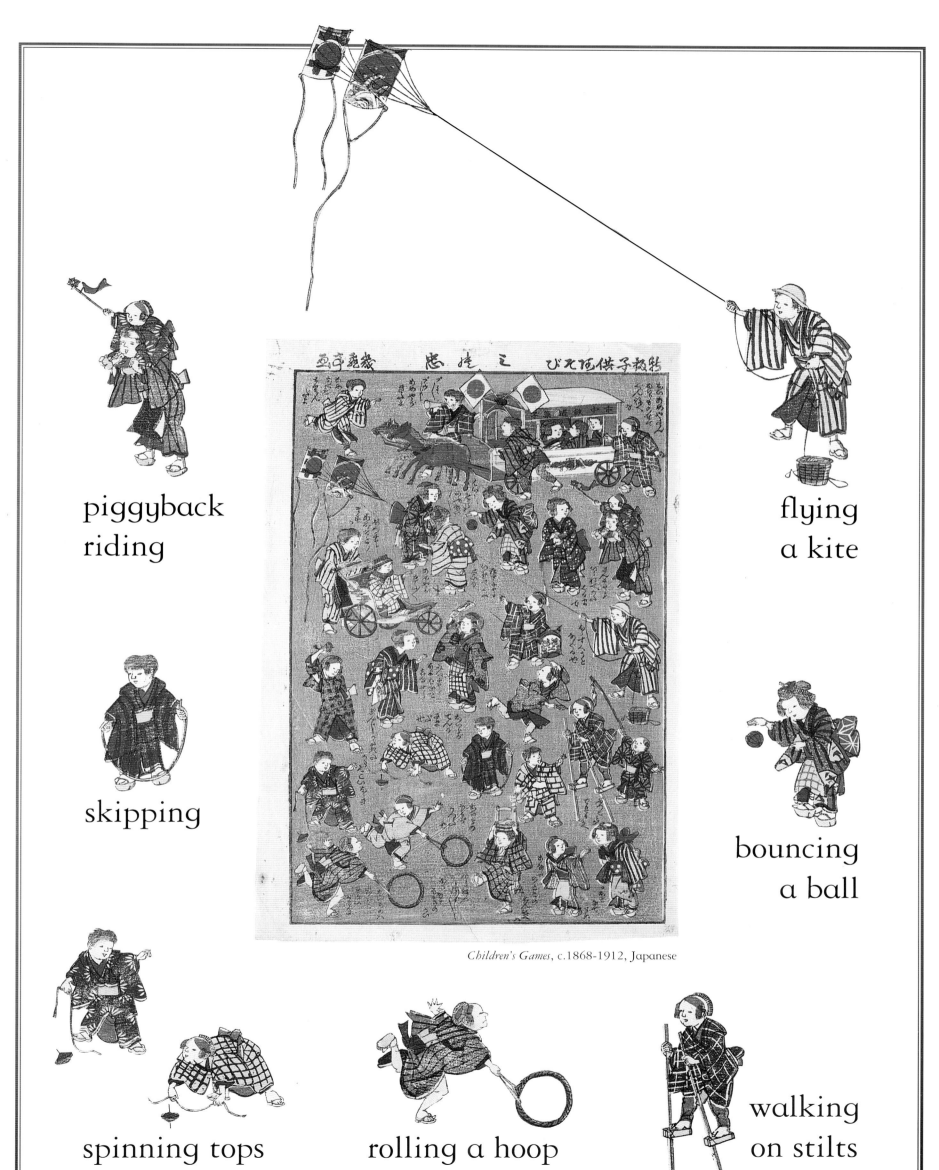

piggyback
riding

flying
a kite

skipping

bouncing
a ball

*Children's Games*, c.1868-1912, Japanese

spinning tops

rolling a hoop

walking
on stilts

# All Dressed Up

chief

*The White Cloud, Head Chief of the Iowas,*
*1844/45, George Catlin*

*Elizabeth I, c.1569, unknown artist*

queen

knights

*Two Knights Armed for the Joust,* after 1561,
from a German tournament book

**soldiers**

*Soldiers of the Tenth Light Dragoons*, 1793, George Stubbs

**shepherdess**

*Shepherd Girl*, c.1778,
George Romney

**clown**

*The White Pierrot*, 1905,
Auguste Renoir

# Where Shall We Live?

*Warwick Castle: the East Front*, 1740s, Canaletto

in a castle

on a country farm

*The Farm*, 1921-22, Joan Miró

in a city apartment

*Study for Cinematic Mural*, Study I, 1939-40, Fernand Léger

# Let's Pretend

to get angry

*The Kabuki Actor Nakamura Shikan II,*
1835, Shunbaisai Hokuei

to be frightened

*Surprised by the Storm,* 1886, Ferdinand Hodler

16

*Women Ironing*, c.1884, Edgar Degas

## to feel tired

*Sleeping Beauty* (detail), 19th century,
Edward Frederick Brewtnall

## to fall asleep

# Make the Faces

**sad**

*St. John Mourning,*
*late 13th century, Circle of Cimabue*

**happy**

*Portrait of Francis Ponge – Hilarious Figure,*
*1947, Jean Dubuffet*

**worried**

*A Kwakiutl Ceremonial Screen,*
*c.1935, Willie Seaweed*

**silly**

*Gorgon's Head, c.490 BC,*
*Greek vase painting*

rude

*Thumbing*, 1991, Gilbert and George

# Animal Noises

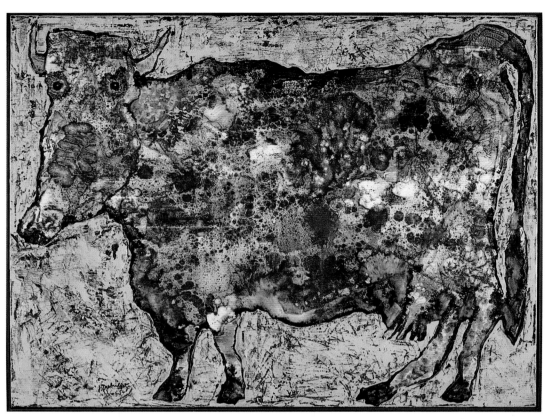

moo like
a cow

*The Cow with the Subtile Nose*, from the *Cows, Grass, Foliage* series, 1954, Jean Dubuffet

neigh like a horse

*Horse Fair*, 1853, Rosa Bonheur

# growl like a tiger

*Tiger by a Torrent*, c.1795, Kishi Ganku

# hoot like an owl

*Drinking cup with owl between two olive twigs,*
*4th century BC, Greek*

# squeak like a mouse

*Fieldmice*, c.1600, Jacob de Gheyn II

# How Do They Smell?

pigsty

*The Pigsty*, 1647,
Paulus Potter

rose

*The Soul of the Rose*, 1908,
John William Waterhouse

old boots

*Boots with Laces*, 1886, Vincent van Gogh

*Thanksgiving*, c.1935, Doris Lee

busy kitchen

# How Do They Taste?

medicine

*The Bitter Drink*, 17th century, Adriaen Brouwer

ice-cream

*Girl Eating Ice-cream*, c.1958, Renato Guttuso

lemons

*Lemons and Citrons*, 1685, Bartolomeo Bimbi

cakes

*Cake Counter*, 1963, Wayne Thiebaud

toothpaste

*First Toothpaste Painting*, 1962, Derek Boshier

# Copy the Patterns

*Three Flags*, 1958, Jasper Johns

stars and stripes

zigzags

*Got a Girl*, 1960-61, Peter Blake

**patchwork**

*The Kiss*, 1907-08, Gustav Klimt

**spots**

*Two Cheetahs*, c.1400, Italian

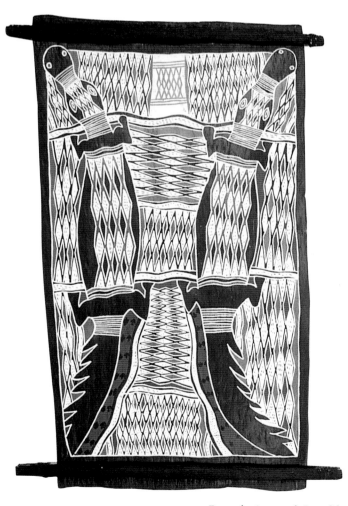

**diamonds**

*Baru the Ancestral Crocodile,* 20th century, Birrpunu Mununggurr

# Touch and Feel

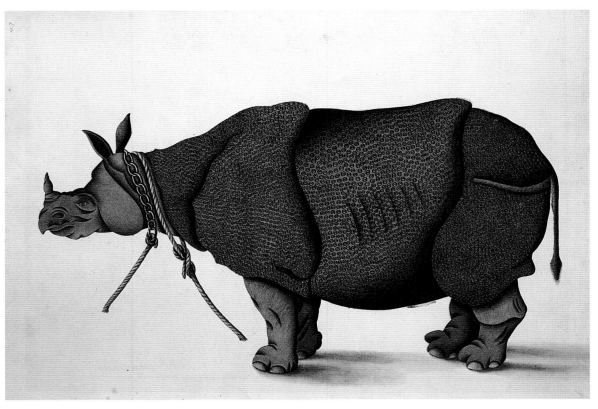

*Indian Rhinoceros*, 18th century, Indian

wrinkly rhino

prickly hedgehogs

*Hedgehogs*, c.1230,
from an English manuscript

furry kitten

*Miss Ann White's Kitten*, 1790, George Stubbs

slimy fish

*Fish on a Blue and White Plate*, 1845, W. B. Gould

# Match the Animals

fox

peacock

hare

birds

horse, pig,
and cow

bats

shark, lobster,
and crab

fish

cockerel

*Creation of the Animals*, c.1380, Master Bertram

# Crazy Creatures

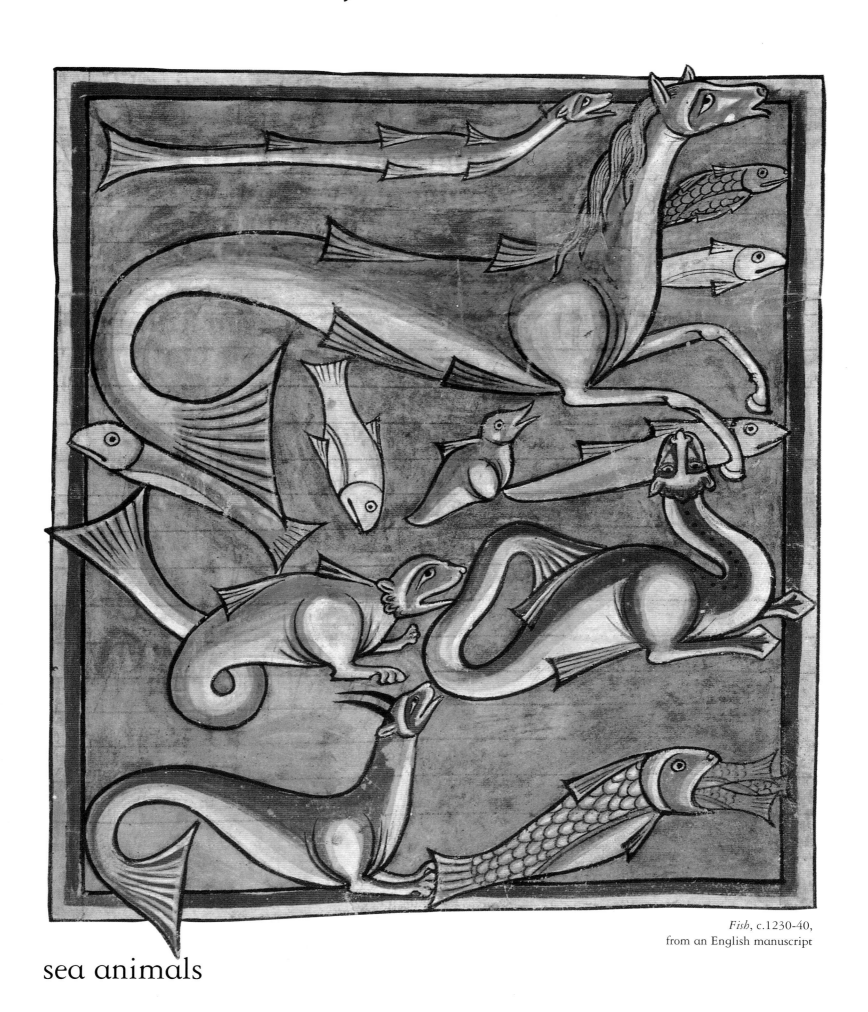

*Fish*, c.1230-40,
from an English manuscript

sea animals

snake

*Snake*, 20th century,
Niki de Saint-Phalle

jaguar

*Jaguar*, c.1300-1500,
Aztec book painting

rhino wolf

*Bahram Gur Slays the Rhino Wolf* (detail), c.1530-35,
from an Iranian manuscript

# Crazy Colours

*The Little Blue Horses*, 1911, Franz Marc

blue horses

yellow
cow

*The Yellow Cow*, 1911, Franz Marc

multicoloured face

*Woman Meditating*, c.1912, Alexei von Jawlensky

# Make up a Story

The girl who turned into a tree

*Apollo and Daphne*, probably 1470-80, Antonio del Pollaiuolo

# The bare-legged soldier

*Captain Thomas Lee*, 1594, Marcus Gheeraerts the Younger

The original stories of these pictures can be found on page 45.

# Spot the Difference

*Vincent's Bedroom in Arles*, 1888, Vincent van Gogh

old bedroom

38

new bedroom

*Bedroom at Arles*, 1992, Roy Lichtenstein

# What Shall We Do Next?

play with toys

*Child with Toys – Gabrielle and the Artist's Son, Jean,*
*c.1894, Auguste Renoir*

run in the park

*The Ball, 1899, Félix Vallotton*

go to the circus

*Bareback Riders*, 1886, W. H. Brown

# Picture List

## Let's Play

10: *Children's Games*, 1560
Pieter Bruegel the Elder, b.1525/30, d.1569,
Netherlandish
oil on wood
118 x 161 cm
Kunsthistorisches Museum, Vienna

11: *Children's Games*, c.1868-1912
Japanese
untreated crepon print from wood blocks
365 x 260 cm
Van Gogh Museum, Amsterdam

## All Dressed Up

12: *The White Cloud, Head Chief of the Iowas*, 1844/45
George Catlin, 1796-1872, American
oil on canvas
71 x 58 cm
National Gallery of Art, Washington, D.C.
Paul Mellon Collection

12: *Elizabeth I*, c.1569
Unknown artist
oil on wood
127.3 x 99.7 cm
National Portrait Gallery, London

12: *Two Knights Armed for the Joust*, after 1561
Manuscript page from an illustrated
tournament book, German
pen and wash on paper
25.1 x 34.6 cm
Metropolitan Museum of Art, New York
The Thomas J. Watson Library

13: *Soldiers of the Tenth Light Dragoons*, 1793
George Stubbs, 1724-1806, British
oil on canvas
102.2 x 127.9 cm
Royal Collection, H.M. Queen Elizabeth II

13: *Shepherd Girl (Little Bo-Peep)*, c.1778
George Romney, 1734-1802, British
oil on canvas
118.1 x 90.2 cm
Philadelphia Museum of Art
The John Howard McFadden Collection

13: *The White Pierrot*, 1905
Auguste Renoir, 1841-1919, French
oil on canvas
81.3 x 62.2 cm
Detroit Institute of Arts
Bequest of Robert H. Tannahill

## Where Shall We Live?

14: *Warwick Castle: the East Front*, 1740s
Canaletto, 1697-1768, Italian
oil on canvas
73 x 122 cm
Birmingham Museums and Art Gallery

14: *The Farm*, 1921-22
Joan Miró, 1893-1983, Spanish
oil on canvas
123.8 x 141.3 cm
National Gallery of Art, Washington, D.C.
Gift of Mary Hemingway

15: *Study for Cinematic Mural*, Study I, 1939-40
Fernand Léger, 1881-1955, French
gouache, brush, pen and ink, and pencil on cardboard
50.7 x 40.5 cm
Museum of Modern Art, New York

## Let's Pretend

16: *The Kabuki Actor Nakamura Shikan II*, 1835
Shunbaisai Hokuei, active c.1824-37, Japanese
colour print from woodblocks
approx. 38 x 25.5 cm
Victoria and Albert Museum, London

16: *Surprised by the Storm*, 1886
Ferdinand Hodler, 1853-1918, Swiss
oil on canvas
100 x 130 cm
Museum Oskar Reinhart am Stadtgarten, Winterthur

17: *Women Ironing*, c.1884
Edgar Degas, 1834-1917, French
pastel
76 x 81 cm
Musée d'Orsay, Paris

17: *Sleeping Beauty* (detail), 19th century
Edward Frederick Brewtnall, 1846-1902, British
oil on canvas
183 x 244 cm
Warrington Museum and Art Gallery, Cheshire
on permanent loan to Walton Hall, Warrington

## Make the Faces

18: *St. John Mourning*, late 13th century
Circle of Cimabue, Italian
oil on canvas on wood
54.4 x 42.5 cm
Städelsches Kunstinstitut, Frankfurt

18: *Portrait of Francis Ponge – Hilarious Figure*, 1947
Jean Dubuffet, 1901-1985, French
moulded plaster painted in oil on canvas
61 x 46 cm
Stedelijk Museum, Amsterdam

18: *A Kwakiutl Ceremonial Screen*, c.1935
Willie Seaweed, 1893-1967, Native North American
paint on cloth
304.8 x 304.8 cm
Private Collection

18: *Gorgon's Head*, c.490 BC
from a red figure hydria (water container), Greek
terracotta
15 x 15.5 cm (image shown)
British Museum, London

19: *Thumbing*, 1991
Gilbert and George, active since 1967, British
photopiece
169 x 142 cm
Private Collection

## Animal Noises

20: *The Cow with the Subtile Nose,* from the
*Cows, Grass, Foliage* series, 1954
Jean Dubuffet, 1901-1985, French
oil and enamel on canvas
88.9 x 116.1 cm
Museum of Modern Art, New York
Benjamin Scharps and David Scharps Fund

20: *Horse Fair*, 1853
Rosa Bonheur, 1822-1899, French
oil on canvas
244.5 x 506.8 cm
Metropolitan Museum of Art, New York
Gift of Cornelius Vanderbilt, 1887

21: *Tiger by a Torrent*, c.1795
Kishi Ganku, 1756-1838, Japanese
hanging scroll, ink and colours on silk
169 x 114.3 cm
British Museum, London

21: *Drinking cup with owl between two olive twigs*,
4th century BC, Greek
terracotta
8.3 x 15.5 cm
City of Stoke-on-Trent Museum and Art Gallery
Staffordshire Polytechnic Collection

21: *Fieldmice*, c.1600
Jacob de Gheyn II, 1565-1629, Dutch
drawing on paper
12.8 x 18.3 cm
Rijksmuseum, Amsterdam

## How Do They Smell?

22: *The Pigsty*, 1647
Paulus Potter, 1625-1654, Dutch
oil on wood
56 x 51 cm
Musées royaux des Beaux-Arts de Belgique, Brussels

22: *The Soul of the Rose*, 1908
John William Waterhouse, 1849-1917, British
oil on canvas
88.3 x 59.1 cm
Private Collection

22: *Boots with Laces*, 1886
Vincent van Gogh, 1853-1890, Dutch
oil on canvas
37.5 x 45 cm
Van Gogh Museum, Amsterdam

23: *Thanksgiving*, c.1935
Doris Lee, 1905-1983, American
oil on canvas
71.4 x 101.6 cm
Art Institute of Chicago
Mr. and Mrs. Frank G. Logan Prize Fund

## How Do They Taste?

24: *The Bitter Drink*, 17th century
Adriaen Brouwer, b.1605/06, d.1638, Flemish
oil on wood
47.5 x 35.5 cm
Städelsches Kunstinstitut, Frankfurt

24: *Girl Eating Ice-cream*, c.1958
Renato Guttuso, 1911-1987, Italian
oil on canvas
71 x 60 cm
Private Collection

24: *Lemons and Citrons*, 1685
Bartolomeo Bimbi, 1648-1730, Italian
oil on canvas
Galleria Palatina, Palazzo Pitti, Florence

25: *Cake Counter*, 1963
Wayne Thiebaud, b.1920, American
oil on canvas
152.4 x 183 cm
Museum Ludwig, Cologne
Ludwig Donation

25: *First Toothpaste Painting*, 1962
Derek Boshier, b.1937, British
oil on canvas
137.4 x 76.5 cm
City Museum and Mappin Art Gallery, Sheffield

## Copy the Patterns

26: *Three Flags*, 1958
Jasper Johns, b.1930, American
encaustic on canvas
78.4 x 115.6 x 12.7 cm
Whitney Museum of American Art, New York
50th Anniversary Gift of the Gilman Foundation, Inc.,
The Lauder Foundation, A. Alfred Taubman, an
anonymous donor, and purchase

26: *Got a Girl*, 1960-61
Peter Blake, b.1932, British
oil, wood, photo-collage, and record on hardboard
92 x 153 cm
Whitworth Art Gallery, University of Manchester

27: *The Kiss*, 1907-08
Gustav Klimt, 1862-1918, Austrian
oil on canvas
180 x 180 cm
Österreichische Galerie, Vienna

27: *Two Cheetahs*, c.1400
Italian
brush and body-colours on parchment
15.6 x 11.5 cm
British Museum, London

27: *Baru the ancestral crocodile at his site in Gumatj country with
the clan diamond design representing fire*, 20th century
Birrpunu Mununggurr, Aboriginal artist of the Gumatj Clan
natural pigments on bark
88 x 48.5 cm
Museum of Mankind, London

## Touch and Feel

28: *Indian Rhinoceros*, 18th century
Indian, a drawing from Marquess Wellesley's
Collection of Natural History Drawings
29 x 42 cm
British Library, London

28: *Hedgehogs*, c.1230
Illustration from a medieval bestiary, English
Royal MS 12 FXIII f.45
vellum
29.8 x 21.4 cm (page size)
approx. 5.5 x 11 cm (image size)
British Library, London

29: *Miss Ann White's Kitten*, 1790
George Stubbs, 1724-1806, British
oil on canvas
25.5 x 30.5 cm
Private Collection

29: *Fish on a Blue and White Plate*, 1845
W. B. Gould, 1803-1853, Australian
oil on canvas
20.3 x 30.5 cm
National Gallery of Australia, Canberra

## Match the Animals

31: *Creation of the Animals*, c.1380
a scene from the Grabower Altarpiece
Master Bertram, active 1367-1410, German
tempera on wood
80 x 51 cm
Kunsthalle, Hamburg

## Crazy Creatures

32: *Fish*, c.1230-40
Illustration from a medieval bestiary, English
MS Harley 4751, f.68
vellum
30.7 x 23.5 cm (page size)
approx. 18 x 15.5 cm (image size)
British Library, London

33: *Snake*, 20th century
Niki de Saint-Phalle, b.1930, French
painted polyester
150 cm (height)
Private Collection

33: *Jaguar*, detail from the Codex Cospi,
one of the sacred painted books
of ancient Mexico, c.1300-1500, Aztec
natural pigments on deerskin
approx. 18 x 18 cm (section), 364 cm (total length)
Biblioteca Universitaria, Bologna

33: *Bahram Gur Slays the Rhino Wolf* (detail), c.1530-35
Illustration from the Shahnama (Book of Kings), Iranian
colours, ink, silver, and gold on paper
28.5 x 18.7 cm
Metropolitan Museum of Art, New York
Gift of Arthur A. Houghton, Jr., 1970

## Crazy Colours

34: *The Little Blue Horses*, 1911
Franz Marc, 1880-1916, German
oil on canvas
61 x 101 cm
Staatsgalerie, Stuttgart
Lutze Collection

34: *The Yellow Cow*, 1911
Franz Marc, 1880-1916, German
oil on canvas
140 x 190 cm
Solomon R. Guggenheim Museum, New York

35: *Woman Meditating*, c.1912
Alexei von Jawlensky, 1864-1941, Russian
oil on board
54 x 48.5 cm
Private Collection

## Make up a Story

36: *Apollo and Daphne*, probably 1470-80
Antonio del Pollaiuolo, c.1432-1498, Italian
oil on wood
29.5 x 20 cm
National Gallery, London

37: *Captain Thomas Lee*, 1594
Marcus Gheeraerts the Younger, b.1561/62, d.1636,
Flemish
oil on canvas
230.5 x 151 cm
Tate Gallery, London

## Spot the Difference

38: *Vincent's Bedroom in Arles*, 1888
Vincent van Gogh, 1853-1890, Dutch
oil on canvas
72 x 90 cm
Van Gogh Museum, Amsterdam

39: *Bedroom at Arles*, 1992
Roy Lichtenstein, b.1923, American
oil and magna on canvas
320 x 420.4 cm
Private Collection

## What Shall We Do Next?

40: *Child with Toys – Gabrielle and the
Artist's Son, Jean*, c.1894
Auguste Renoir, 1841-1919, French
oil on canvas
54.3 x 65.4 cm
National Gallery of Art, Washington, D.C.
Collection of Mr. and Mrs. Paul Mellon

40: *The Ball*, 1899
Félix Vallotton, 1865-1925, Swiss
oil on card on wood
48 x 61 cm
Musée d'Orsay, Paris

41: *Bareback Riders*, 1886
W. H. Brown, active 1886-87, American
oil on cardboard mounted on wood
47 x 62.2 cm
National Gallery of Art, Washington, D.C.
Gift of Edgar William and Bernice Chrysler Garbisch

## Front Cover

From top left; clockwise:
*The White Cloud, Head Chief of the Iowas* (detail), page 12
*Miss Ann White's Kitten* (detail), page 29
*Children's Games* (detail), page 11
*Hedgehogs* (detail), page 28
*Bareback Riders* (detail), page 41
*Child with Toys - Gabrielle and the Artist's Son, Jean* (detail), page 40
*Gorgon's Head*, page 18
*Fish*, page 32

## Front Flap

*Miss Ann White's Kitten* (detail), page 29
*Two Cheetahs* (detail), page 27

## Back Cover

From top left; clockwise:
*Soldiers of the Tenth Light Dragoons* (detail), page 13
*Miss Ann White's Kitten* (detail), page 29
*Children's Games* (detail), page 11
*Shepherd Girl* (detail), page 13
*The White Pierrot* (detail), page 13

## Title Page

*Bahram Gur Slays the Rhino Wolf*, page 33
*Miss Ann White's Kitten* (detail), page 29
*Hedgehogs*, page 28

## Contents

*Fieldmice* (detail), page 21
*Two Knights Armed for the Joust*, page 12
*Women Ironing* (detail), page 17
*Fieldmice* (detail), page 21
*The Bitter Drink* (detail), page 24
*Two Cheetahs* (detail), page 27
*The Little Blue Horses*, page 34
*Apollo and Daphne* (detail), page 36
*Bareback Riders*, page 41

## Note to Parents and Teachers

*The Kabuki Actor Nakamura Shikan II* (detail), page 16
*Gorgon's Head*, page 18
*Thanksgiving*, page 23
*Vincent's Bedroom in Arles*, page 38
*The Soul of the Rose*, page 22
*Drinking cup with owl between two olive twigs*, page 21
*Horse Fair*, page 20

The author and publisher would like to thank the museums, galleries, and collectors listed for their kind permission to reproduce the pictures in this book.

### Make up a Story

These are the stories of the paintings on pages 36 and 37.

### Apollo and Daphne

There are many different versions of the story of Apollo and Daphne. This version is based on the story accompanying the painting in the National Gallery.

Cupid, the god of love, fired one of his golden arrows at the sun god, Apollo. This made Apollo fall desperately in love with a young girl called Daphne. But one day Apollo annoyed Cupid by questioning his skill with a bow and arrow. Cupid was determined to seek revenge.

He fired a blunted arrow at Daphne which made her dislike Apollo. She ran away from him through a forest and down towards a river. Just as Apollo caught up with her, she cried out to her father, the river god, for help. Her father heard her and turned her into a beautiful laurel tree, so Apollo could never catch her.

### Captain Thomas Lee

Thomas Lee was a captain in the army of Queen Elizabeth I. He was a brave and ambitious man but often in trouble. In 1594 he had this unusual portrait painted and sent to the queen.

The painting was full of messages to her. There is some Latin writing in the oak tree which means "to act and suffer bravely". This was to remind the queen of his own bravery and suffering. His beautiful shirt and finely engraved helmet and pistol show that he was a man of noble birth. But his bare legs, like those of a poor Irish foot soldier, seem to suggest that he could not afford a pair of trousers.

Captain Lee hoped the queen would reward him for the time he had spent fighting in Ireland. He wanted money, land, and power. But his scheme failed. Seven years later he was executed for plotting against the queen.

# Acknowledgments

**Key**: l=left, r=right, t=top, c=centre, a=above, b=below

The author and publisher would like to thank the following for their permission to reproduce the photographs:

**front cover**
tl: © 1996 Board of Trustees, National Gallery of Art, Washington
cla: © By permission of The British Library
cl: Michael Holford
tc: Roy Miles Gallery, 29 Bruton Street, London W1/Bridgeman Art Library, London
bc: © 1996 Board of Trustees, National Gallery of Art, Washington
tr: © Van Gogh Museum (Vincent van Gogh Foundation), Amsterdam
cra: © By permission of The British Library
cr: © 1996 Board of Trustees, National Gallery of Art, Washington

**front flap**
tc: Roy Miles Gallery, 29 Bruton Street, London W1/Bridgeman Art Library, London
bc: © British Museum

**back cover**
tl: © Her Majesty Queen Elizabeth II, The Royal Collection
bl: © 1986 The Detroit Institute of Arts
tc: Roy Miles Gallery, 29 Bruton Street, London W1/Bridgeman Art Library, London
tr: © Van Gogh Museum (Vincent van Gogh Foundation), Amsterdam
br: © Philadelphia Museum of Art

4: © The Metropolitan Museum of Art, New York
5bc: © By permission of The British Library
6t: © 1991 The Metropolitan Museum of Art, New York
6bl: © Rijksmuseum, Amsterdam
6br: © photo RMN
7tl: © Rijksmuseum, Amsterdam
7tr: © Staatsgalerie, Stuttgart
7cl: Artothek
7cr: © Reproduced by courtesy of the Trustees, The National Gallery, London
7bl: © British Museum
7br: © 1996 Board of Trustees, National Gallery of Art, Washington

8tl: © By courtesy of the Board of Trustees of The Victoria & Albert Museum
8cr: Michael Holford
8bl: © 1995, The Art Institute of Chicago. All rights reserved.
9tr: © Van Gogh Museum (Vincent van Gogh Foundation), Amsterdam
9cl: Roy Miles Gallery, 29 Bruton Street, London W1/Bridgeman Art Library, London
9cr: et archive
9bl: © The Metropolitan Museum of Art, New York
10: © Kunsthistorisches Museum, Vienna
11: © Van Gogh Museum (Vincent van Gogh Foundation), Amsterdam
12tl: © 1996 Board of Trustees, National Gallery of Art, Washington
12tr: By courtesy of the National Portrait Gallery, London
12b: © 1991 The Metropolitan Museum of Art, New York
13t: © Her Majesty Queen Elizabeth II, The Royal Collection
13bl: © Philadelphia Museum of Art
13br: © 1986 The Detroit Institute of Arts
14t: © Birmingham Museums and Art Gallery
14b: © ADAGP, Paris and DACS, London 1996 /Board of Trustees, National Gallery of Art, Washington
15: © SPADEM/ADAGP, Paris and DACS, London 1996/1995 The Museum of Modern Art, New York
16t: © By courtesy of the Board of Trustees of The Victoria & Albert Museum
16b: © Museum Oskar Reinhart Am Stadtgarten
17t: © photo RMN
17b: © Warrington Museum & Art Gallery, Cheshire/Bridgeman Art Library, London
18tl: © Ursula Edelman
18tr: © ADAGP, Paris and DACS, London 1996/Stedelijk Museum, Amsterdam
18bl: Christies, New York
18br: Michael Holford
19: courtesy Anthony d'Offay Gallery, London
20t: © ADAGP, Paris and DACS, London 1996/1995 The Museum of Modern Art, New York
20b: © 1986 The Metropolitan Museum of Art, New York
21tl: © British Museum
21cr: et archive
21b: © Rijksmuseum, Amsterdam
22tl: © Musées royaux des Beaux-Arts de Belgique
22tr: Roy Miles Gallery, 29 Bruton Street, London W1/Bridgeman Art Library, London

22b: © Van Gogh Museum (Vincent van Gogh Foundation), Amsterdam
23: © 1995, The Art Institute of Chicago. All Rights Reserved.
24tl: Artothek
24tr: © DACS 1996/Scala
24b: Scala
25t: © Rheinisches Bildarchiv, Köln
25b: © Reproduced by permission of Sheffield Arts and Museums Department
26t: © Jasper Johns/DACS, London/VAGA, New York 1996/Whitney Museum of American Art, New York
26b: © The Whitworth Art Gallery, The University of Manchester
27t: Artothek
27bl, 27br: © British Museum
28t, 28b: © By permission of The British Library
29t: Roy Miles Gallery, 29 Bruton Street, London W1/Bridgeman Art Library, London
29b: © National Gallery of Australia, Canberra
30, 31: Elke Walford, Fotowerkstatt, Kunsthalle, Hamburg
32: © By permission of The British Library
33tr: © ADAGP, Paris and DACS, London 1996/Christies, Amsterdam
33l: Werner Forman Archive
33br: © 1995 The Metropolitan Museum of Art, New York
34t: Staatsgalerie, Stuttgart
34b: Artothek
35: © DACS 1996/Scala
36: © Reproduced by courtesy of the Trustees, The National Gallery, London
37: © Tate Gallery, London
38t, 38bl: © Van Gogh Museum (Vincent van Gogh Foundation), Amsterdam
39t, 39bl: © Roy Lichtenstein/DACS 1996
40t: © 1996 Board of Trustees, National Gallery of Art, Washington
40b: © photo RMN
41: © 1996 Board of Trustees, National Gallery of Art, Washington